Oh, The Sh!t You'll Pack
Text by: L.G. Breuer
Illustrations by: Tais Krymova
Copyright © 2021 by L.G. Breuer
All rights reserved
Summary: A savvy world traveler quickly learns
what it means to travel with kids.
"You don't get a vacation, you get change of scenery"
My mom, on travelling with kids

ISBN 978-0-578-93581-2 (paperback)
ISBN 978-1-7375070-0-0 (trade)

To Oskar and Alva, for helping reset
expectations on what packing entails.

To Anjulee, for summing up travelling
with kids in 5 quick words.

S o you're off on vacation,

Hip hip hooray!
Pack up your bag
And you're on your way!

Call a taxi, take your car or hop on the bus.
Nothing can stop your wanderlust.

Breeze through the airport and stop for coffee,
No lines for you and your TSA Pre.

But wait, what is this? You have children you say?
It's no longer that easy to get away.

So, I'm sorry to tell you, I take it all back.
Here's a short list of all the things you will pack.

OH, THE SHIT

YOU WILL PACK!

The stroller, the diaper bag, the child's car seat.
Their pajamas, the crib, don't forget the crib sheet.

Their lovie, their binkie and a few extra swaddles.
Their bib, baby formula and a set of glass bottles.

Baby monitor, high chair and a few plastic baggies,
Some for wet clothes and all of their soiled nappies.

Diapers, wet wipes, and organic butt cream,
A thermometer, Tylenol and baby sunscreen.

Band aids, nose frida, the nebulizer,
Disinfectant wipes and hand sanitizer.

Sunhat, swim diapers, mittens or warm jacket,
If ever in doubt, say fuck it and pack it.

Don't forget to pack clothes, some sock and some shoes.
An assembly of outfits for the vacation you choose.

Then pack a few extras and multiple it by three,
They require more outfits than an award show emcee.

Hooded towel, travel tub, toothbrush and toothpaste.
Better wrap up this packing, get going, make haste!

Their favorite shirt that you don't really like?
Might as well pack it, no need for a fight.

Is this vacation even worth it, you might begin to ask,
after making a list of all of the shit you will pack.

Toys for the plane, toys for the car.
Pack too few and you won't get far.

Shampoo, baby carrier, picture books by the stack.
Is there anything left you haven't yet packed?

Pack enough snacks to feed a small army.
Better to be safe than hungry and sorry.

A bottle of wine to help you relax,
You're already exhausted by all the shit you've packed.

Have more than one?
Multiply this by two.

It doesn't get easier,
just a bigger to-do.

Do you have everything?
Now stop and think.

Oh what the hell, might as well pack the sink.

One bag, two bag, three bag, four.
Fingers crossed you still fit through the door.

Out to the car and the puzzle begins.
How will you fit all of the shit you've packed in?

Start with the trunk, now it barely closes.
The rest at your feet and up to your noses.

How does such a small child take up so much car space!
Your old ways of traveling have left without trace.

Go for one month, a week or a day.
The shit you will pack always remains the same.

Traveling alone doesn't mean you're shit free. You will still pack your guilt with a dash of anxiety.

Leaving your child at home
while you travel?!
Surely, in your absence,
the house will unravel.

But even with all of the shit you will pack,
There is always one thing you can count on for fact.

And that is the love of your little world traveler,
Because kids are the gift that makes life spectacular.

They will one day appreciate all that you do,
When they have their own kids and
have to pack for them too.

So until you discover a much needed
life hack, on how to avoid all of
the shit you will pack.

Learn to love the chaos and try to remain strong.
And enjoy these moments, they soon will be gone.

Congratulations on your bundle of joy and the next big adventure.

CPSIA information can be obtained
at www.ICGtesting.com
Printed in the USA
BVHW020713090921
615465BV00006B/36